BREAKTHROUGH

GENETICS

Tony Hooper

SIMON & SCHUSTER
YOUNG BOOKS

A ZOË BOOK

© 1992 Zoë Books Limited

Devised and produced by
Zoë Books Limited
15 Worthy Lane
Winchester
Hampshire SO23 7AB
England

First published in Great Britain in 1992 by
Simon and Schuster Young Books
Campus 400, Maylands Avenue
Hemel Hempstead
Hertfordshire HP2 7EZ

ISBN 0 7500 10207

A catalogue record for this book is available from the British Library

Printed in Great Britain by BPCC Hazell Books, Paulton and Aylesbury

Design: Pardoe Blacker
Picture research: Sarah Staples
Illustrations: Arcana; Sallie Alane Reason

Photograph acknowledgements

The publishers wish to acknowledge. with thanks, the following photographic sources:

4l Mary Evans Picture Library; 4r, 5t, 5b ZEFA; 6 Ann Ronan; 7l, 7r Mary Evans Picture Library; 8 Ann Ronan; 11t Mary Evans Picture Library; 11r Rex Features; 12 Mary Evans Picture Library; 13t NHPA; 14r Hulton Picture Company; 16 Mary Evans Picture Library; 17 London Features International; 18l Mary Evans Picture Library; 18r Ann Ronan; 20, 23b, 24, 25l Science Photo Library; 26 Genetics Society of America; 27b Hulton Picture Company; 28 Science Photo Library; 29t Magnum Photos; 29b Trevor Hill; 30b, 31, 33t Science Photo Library; 36 A Bishop/Genus; 37 NHPA; 39t Unilever; 39b Science Photo Library; 40l, 40r Frank Spooner; 41 Science Photo Library; 42, 43 Frank Spooner

GENETICS

CONTENTS

WHAT IS SCIENCE?

Science is the study of how living things and the universe work. In early times, people worked things out by discussion and guess-work. In Ancient Greece, thinkers, or philosophers, discussed many aspects of life. They believed that any question could be answered by reasoning alone. However, they could only guess at how things worked as they did not have any way to prove their ideas were correct. Many of the ideas that they thought were true were later discovered to be quite wrong. However, until these discoveries were made, many of their ideas, or **theories**, were the basis of 'science' for thousands of years.

The child's red hair is inherited from her mother (on the right). The gene that causes red hair can miss a generation. This explains why parents who do not have red hair can have a red-haired child.

ARISTOTLE

Aristotle was one of the greatest of the Ancient Greek philosophers. He lived from 384 BC to 322 BC. He thought that children were made by something he called 'the substance', which was found in women, and 'the form', which came from men. The form and the substance did not mix together but the form had a magical influence on the substance. Aristotle also believed that living things gradually changed from plants, through animals, to end in the highest form – humanity. This was the first time the idea of **evolution**, changing from one form to another, had been recorded.

QUESTIONS AND ANSWERS

Gradually scientists began to separate the different areas of interest and give them different names. One of these branches of science is now called genetics. This is the study of **heredity** or how some plants and animals remain similar from **generation** to generation while others change. The study of genetics came about when people began asking How is life created? and How do groups of the same or similar plants and animals come into being?

GENETICS

BREAKTHROUGH AND INSIGHT

Science often appears to progress in a series of sudden discoveries. These breakthroughs often change people's way of thinking completely.

However, breakthroughs are only possible against a background of careful observation and thought from other people. This is true even when a chance observation leads to an **insight**, or an idea about how things might be connected.

Many of these children come from different ethnic backgrounds, or from different races. We can often recognise what race children are from by the shape of their face or eyes, and from the colour of their skin and hair.

Harvest time on the Canadian prairies. Cereal crops have been improved by genetic engineering to give higher yields and to have improved resistance to disease.

GENETICS

Over many years, the study of genetics has made many amazing discoveries. One of these was how information which affected the appearance or behaviour of plants and animals was passed on to the next generation.

Scientists found a substance in living material which they called **deoxyribonucleic acid**, known as **DNA** for short. About 50 years ago scientists discovered that this substance was important in passing on the genetic information. Since then, by working with DNA, scientists have been able to make changes that have improved people's health and their food crops. Further **experiments** are finding new ways of using DNA.

WHAT IS SCIENCE?

THE CHURCH AND SCIENCE

During the Middle Ages, the Christian religion gradually become very powerful in Europe. The leaders of the Christian Church controlled all the ideas and beliefs and did not allow anyone to have ideas that were different. They ran all the schools and so controlled the spread of knowledge. Only a few people were allowed to read and write.

The Church taught that God created everything at once over seven days, and that he controlled everything that happened in the universe. If anyone questioned this teaching they could be tortured or killed.

The Spanish Inquisition put people to death by burning after they had been tortured and convicted of heresy. The victim here has been made to wear an overall painted with figures of demons and creatures supposed to come from Hell.

T·I·M·E · L·I·N·E

6000 BC
In Asia Minor, people observed that there were features passed from parent to child. A carving from the city of Chaldea shows distinctive features on the manes of horses and their foals.

500 BC
Ancient Greek society produced great thinkers such as Aristotle. These philosophers started the beginnings of science when they thought about people and their environment.

AD 1100-1400
Christianity was very strong throughout Europe and all teaching and knowledge was strictly controlled by the Church. No one was allowed to question any of the beliefs that the Church said were 'true'.

SEEKING KNOWLEDGE

From the 1400s, the control of the Church weakened. People became much more interested in learning and many universities and new schools were set up. This period saw the first stirrings of what we now call science, but it still depended very much on the ideas of the Ancient Greeks. These ideas were widely accepted until well into the 1500s. From 1500 to 1700, people began to carry out tests, or experiments, to prove that their ideas were right. These experiments were carefully recorded and the idea of a scientific method developed.

GENETICS

1400-1600

The power of the Church was reduced. A new thirst for knowledge led to great developments in inventions and thoughts about people and their environment. The invention of the printing press in the 1450s allowed knowledge to be spread more widely.

1700-1800

The Church was no longer able to punish people who questioned its teaching. However, its teachings were still widely believed and social pressure was very powerful in controlling new ideas.

In the 1600s William Harvey carried out many experiments. He proved that blood flowed around the body. He also proved that the unborn embryo in deer grew larger and more complex as the pregnancy progressed. This idea about an embryo was not new as it had been mentioned in the Koran – the holy book of the Muslims – nearly 1000 years before. However, the results of Harvey's experiments were not accepted until the 1700s.

Science as we know it dates from the 1600s when Isaac Newton began to make carefully recorded experiments to prove his ideas. Newton was a brilliant scientist and explored many areas of science, particularly those of mathematics and physics.

THE CHURCH AND SCIENCE

EARLY IDEAS

In the 1700s, the German scientist Caspar Wolff proved that the theory of preformationism was wrong. He carried out experiments which showed that plants and animals grew from material that, at the start, appeared to be nothing like the final plant or animal. From his work on embryos Wolff then produced the theory of **epigenesis** which supposed that all the missing material must grow during the development period.

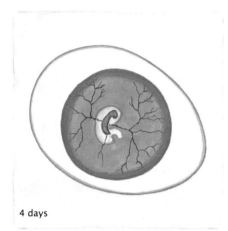

4 days

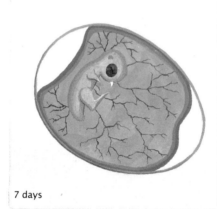

7 days

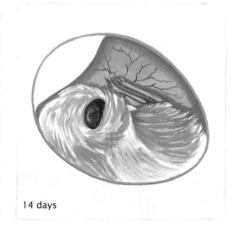

14 days

19 days

hatching

the young chick

The development of this chick embryo shows that the feathers, claws and neck are not preformed, but gradually develop as the embryo matures.

MYSTERY OR SCIENCE?

The force that caused the embryo to grow was not understood and many believed that it was caused by some mystical or even magical force. The 1700s was a time when scientific thought was still dominated by widely-held religious beliefs.

However, this did not satisfy the growing band of scientists who were seeking more **rational** explanations.

In the 1800s, in Russia, Karl von Baer developed the idea that the material, or **tissue**, of the embryo gradually changed from a simple to a more complex form.

GENETICS

FIXITY OF THE SPECIES

The theory that all species were fixed was put forward by the Swedish botanist Carolus Linnaeus. This theory was widely held during the 1700s and 1800s and is still proposed by some people today. The problem with the theory of species being fixed is that there is no way to explain the small differences or variations that can be seen within the same species. By the end of the 1700s, some people began to doubt this theory and an alternative, the theory of transformation, began to take its place.

PRIMAL FILAMENT

At the end of the 1700s Erasmus Darwin, an English physican, put forward the idea of a primal filament or continuous thread which passed to each generation. This filament was able to acquire new parts and improvements which it could pass on to the next generation. The improvements were thought to come from the organism's efforts to adjust to changes in habitat, climate or diet over several generations.

This American rockstar, Edgar Winter, has a rare genetic condition called albinoism, which means that he has no pigment. His hair and skin are perfectly white and his eyes are pink. Albinoism is an example of a mutation, so the children of albinos are likely to be albinos too.

THE THEORY OF TRANSFORMATION

This theory suggested that all known groups or genera were, at first, a few basic types. From these basic types, all the different species had come as a result of variations in environment. The first to propose the idea of transformation were the Frenchmen, Comte de Buffon and Pierre de Maupertuis in 1754. However, their ideas were directly against the teaching of the Church. Maupertuis thought that in reproduction, tiny particles of sperm combined. If this happened correctly, normal young were born. When they combined incorrectly or abnormally, new species could be made. These abnormalities are now known as mutations.

THE LAW OF SEGREGATION

From his experiments, Johann Mendel thought that each male or female parent must have two factors which defined a character (such as height), and each parent gave only one factor to its offspring. When the sex cells, or gametes, are formed the factors are split and given, by chance, to the offspring.

The results of Mendel's experiments have been proved time and again by others, and his law is the foundation of modern genetics. Mendel was able, because of his wide education in philosophy, mathematics and biology, to take an ordered, or systematic, approach to explain the role of hybrids in forming new species.

These corns have been genetically developed to emphasize different characteristics like thickness, length, colour, and the number of grains on the cob.

PROVING MENDEL'S LAW

Although Mendel made his work public in 1865, it was not until 1900, sixteen years after Mendel had died, that three other scientists, Erik von Tschermak in Austria, Carl Correns in Germany and Hugo de Vries in Holland, all arrived at the same conclusions independently. All ·of them accepted that Mendel's work was the breakthrough, and it stands today as one of the most important biological discoveries of all time.

GENETICS

BLACK PANTHERS

A good example of Mendel's law of segregation is the black panther, which is a variety of the spotted leopard. When the black and spotted cats are freely interbred in zoos, the F1 cats are all spotted and the F2 leopards are – as Mendel's first law predicts – three spotted leopards for each black panther.

The spotted leopard has the dominant characteristic. The black panther is a variety of spotted leopard resulting from the recessive factor.

Spotted leopards and black panthers

spotted leopard

black panther

F1
all spotted

spotted leopards
breed

F2 leopards and panthers in the ratio of 3:1

The black panther is more common in dense, dark forests where its colouring allows it to hide in the darker areas more easily. On the plains, the black panther is rarer because it is too easily seen by its prey.

THE LAW OF SEGREGATION

THE BUILDING BLOCKS OF LIFE

By the end of the 1800s, many important discoveries had been made about the basic tissue of living things. Scientists had discovered that this material was built up of small units they called **cells**. All living things start life as a single fertilized cell, called a **zygote**. This single-celled zygote splits into two and begins to multiply to make the building blocks of plants or animals. When studying cells scientists had identified threads in the core, or **nucleus**, of the cells. They called the individual threads **chromosomes**.

The cells of plants and animals look different superficially, but their construction and operation are very similar. They both have a nucleus in their core which is surrounded by a cytoplasm.

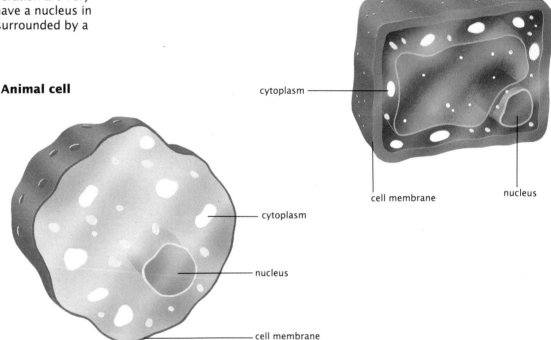

Plant cell

cytoplasm

cell membrane

nucleus

Animal cell

cytoplasm

nucleus

cell membrane

APPEARANCES CAN BE DECEPTIVE

In 1905 another important discovery was made by the Danish botanist Wilhelm Johannsen. He discovered that cells contained factors that were connected with heredity. Johannsen was the first to make a distinction between the appearance or phenotype of an individual and its hidden hereditary make-up or genotype. The phenotype was the result of the individual's response to the environment. For example, a dwarf pea will look different if poorly watered when compared to its identical genotype that has been grown in ideal conditions.

THE EFFECTS OF ENVIRONMENT

In 1869 another scientist, Sir Francis Galton who was a cousin of Charles Darwin, put forward the idea that as identical twins have exactly the same inherited make-up, then any differences between them must be due to differences in their environment.

Galton's special interests lay in the inheritance of physical characteristics and special talents. He studied wrestlers and their families in the North of England to see if any of their characteristics or skills were passed on to the next generation.

Galton discovered that fingerprints are unique to an individual, and so laid the foundations for solving criminal cases by identifying the fingerprint.

A group of human chromosomes. The pinched-in area down the middle is called the centromere. When the chromosome divides, it splits length-wise at the centromere.

EUGENICS

Francis Galton was also responsible for the idea that animals and humans could be improved by selective breeding. This became known as eugenics. These ideas were later misused by Adolf Hitler in Nazi Germany. Hitler attempted to create what he called a 'master-race'. However, the study of eugenics is now concerned with eliminating inherited diseases.

These genetically identical twins grew from a zygote which split in two. Identical twins are often studied to see how different environments affect them.

THE BUILDING BLOCKS OF LIFE

CHROMOSOMES

During the 1800s the German zoologist Theodor Boveri and another scientist called Henking had shown that when cells divided, both cells had an exact copy of the number and type of chromosomes in their nucleus. This process was called **mitosis**. The single cell divides into two, then four, then eight and so on. Each cell contains a complete set of chromosomes. All the cells of an organism will contain the same number of chromosomes. In humans this is 46. The chromosomes occur in pairs.

A cell during the last stage of mitosis. The two genetically identical daughter cells are still connected by threads of cytoplasm.

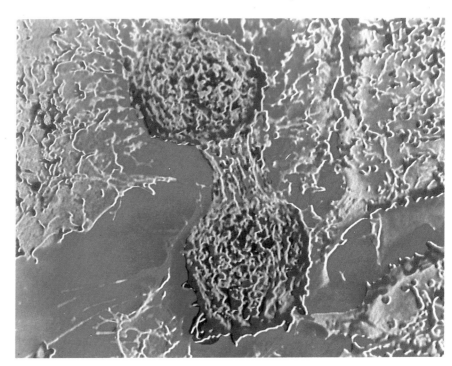

THE GAMETES

There is another kind of cell division called **meiosis**. It occurs only in the reproductive organs where the gametes or sex cells are formed. For example, in the human body 23 chromosomes are found in a female egg and 23 are found in a male sperm. When these cells fuse together to form a zygote during reproduction, the zygote then has the full amount of 46 chromosomes in 23 matching pairs. The members of each pair of chromosomes are called **homologues**.

THE SEX CHROMOSOME

One member of each homologue comes from the father while the other comes from the mother. There are two types of chromosome: those concerned with sex determination, or **sex chromosomes**, and the rest, which are called **autosomes**.

Henking is credited with discovering the difference between the types in 1891. The sex determining chromosome was named the **X chromosome** because biologists were still uncertain about its precise behaviour. However, in humans as well as most animals, both males and females have two sex determining chromosomes. In women they are both X chromosomes but in men there is one X and another, smaller, **Y chromosome**.

THE CHROMOSOME THEORY OF INHERITANCE

When Mendel's discoveries were brought to the attention of scientists studying cell development, they observed the similarities in his results and the results of studies with chromosomes in cell division.

Walter Sutton, an American biologist, knew Mendel's work on pea hybrids and was the first to suggest that chromosomes held the hereditary factors everyone was looking for. In 1902 he published his *Chromosome Theory of Inheritance*.

In meiosis the 46 chromosomes in the female and male both split into two groups. Each set of cells contains 23 chromosomes. When a female (egg) set combines with the male (sperm) set, fertilization occurs. The fertilized egg contains the full set of chromosomes.

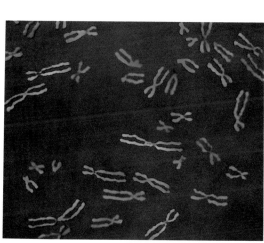

These chromosomes are from a healthy human female. They are shown in the last stage before cell division takes place. There are 46 chromosomes in each cell in 22 matched pairs, plus one sex-determining pair.

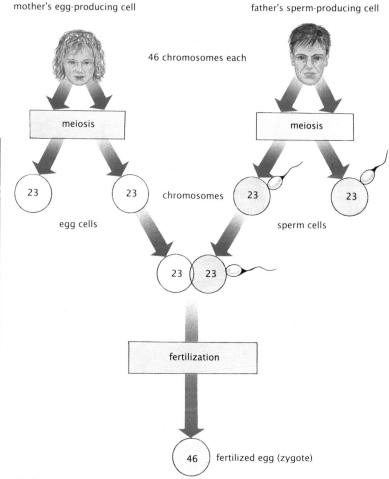

mother's egg-producing cell

father's sperm-producing cell

46 chromosomes each

meiosis

meiosis

23

23

chromosomes

23

23

egg cells

sperm cells

23

23

fertilization

46

fertilized egg (zygote)

Meiosis in sexual reproduction

CHROMOSOMES

SOLVING THE PUZZLE

With any breakthrough, several pieces of research often need to be fitted together like a puzzle. Scientists already knew what DNA was made of (its components) how the bases were always present in the same amounts (Chargaff's rules), and what DNA looked like (its shape) when it was photographed using X-rays. But no-one could explain how all of these things were related.

Biological matter is mainly made up of these six types of atom. They are shown in models as coloured balls. These atoms join together in various combinations to make up molecules of other substances.

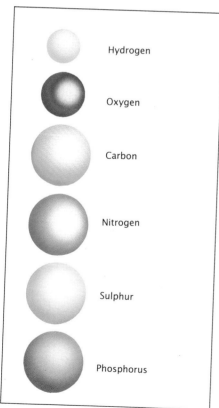

Hydrogen

Oxygen

Carbon

Nitrogen

Sulphur

Phosphorus

THE COMPONENTS OF DNA

In 1909, the American biochemist Phoebus Levene and others had been involved with studying the basic structure of DNA and making a **chemical analysis**. Their work had shown that DNA was made up from three basic components:

a sugar
an acid (phosphoric acid)
an organic **base**:
    adenine (A)   thymine (T)
    guanine (G)   cytosine (C)

The four different bases fall into two groups called:

purines   = A and G
pyrimidines = T and C

CHARGAFF'S RULES

In 1949, the Austro-American biochemist Erwin Chargaff extended this work when he found that DNA taken from several species had the same basic composition. He discovered that the amounts of the purine base A was always the same as the amount of the pyrimidine base T. Similarly there were always equal amounts of bases G and C.

These results are known as Chargaff's Rules, and they made it clear that there were some rules which controlled the arrangement of the bases within the DNA.

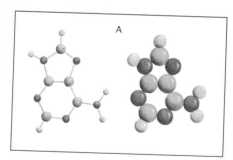

A

purines

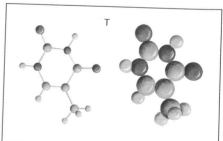

T

pyrimidines

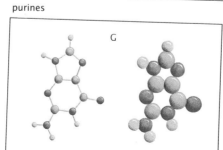

G

C

GENETICS

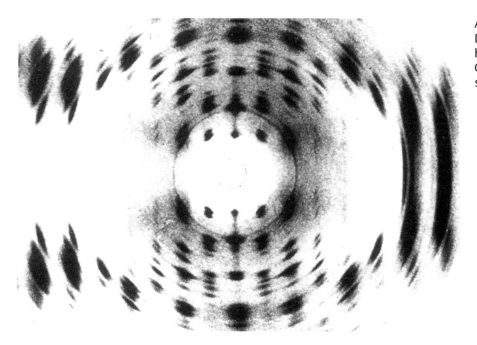

An X-ray diffraction picture of the DNA molecule. An image like this helped James Watson and Francis Crick to unravel the double helix structure of DNA.

THE SHAPE

In 1953 at King's College in London, Maurice Wilkins and Rosalind Franklin were working on passing X-rays through DNA. When X-rays are passed through DNA the rays are scattered. These resulting X-ray diffraction patterns give clues about the physical arrangement of the particles making up DNA. Wilkins and Franklin's results were recorded on film and the photograph showed that DNA was a long, thin molecule coiled in a spiral, or **helix**.

THE DOUBLE HELIX

James Watson and Francis Crick of the Cavendish Laboratory in Cambridge, England used all of these pieces of information to solve the puzzle in 1953. Watson and Crick thought that Chargaff's Rules probably meant that base A was always paired with base T and that base G was always paired with base C. This could only happen if DNA was made up from two strands twisted together to form a 'double helix'.

They built a model which showed that the DNA molecule could be thought of as being a ladder where the bases form the rungs and the sugar and phosphoric acid make up the two sides. The sides are then twisted to make the double-helix.

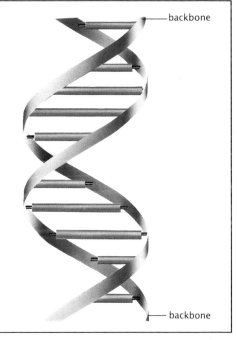

backbone

backbone

SOLVING THE PUZZLE

KEY DATES

1665 Robert Hooke discovers the cell

1754 Pierre Maupertuis suggests species transform over time

1802 Jean-Baptiste Lamarck gives biology its name

1809 Lamarck's book *Philosophie zoologique* published

1824 René Dutrochet discovers that tissue is made from living cells

1831 Charles Darwin sets out on his voyage on the *Beagle*

1833 Robert Brown discovers the cell nucleus

1858 Charles Darwin publishes his results

1859 Darwin publishes *On the Origin of Species by Natural Selection*

1865 Gregor Mendel discovers the laws of segregation

1868 Freidrich Miescher discovers nuclein, later renamed DNA

1888 G Waldyer names the 'chromosome'

1891 Henking describes sex chromosomes and autosomes

1901 Hugo de Vries first describes mutations

1902 Walter Sutton publishes the *Chromosome Theory of Inheritance*

1907 First culture 'in vitro' of animal cells by R Harrison

1909 Wilhelm Johannsen first uses the name 'gene' and Garrod suggests that errors in genes lead to hereditary disorders

1910 Thomas Hunt Morgan discovers the sex-linked gene

1926 Morgan's book, *The Theory of the Gene,* published

1927 Hermann Muller shows that X-rays cause mutation

1937 Richard Goldschmidt discovers genes exist as points along the chromosome

1944 Avery, MacCarty, and Macleod suggest that DNA is involved in the hereditary material

1950 Chargaff's Rules established about the basic chemistry of DNA

1952 Hershey and Chase prove that DNA is the hereditary material, and Wilkins and Franklin take X-ray diffraction pictures of DNA

1953 Crick and Watson discover the structure of DNA

1957 Arthur Kronberg shows the 'unzipping' of DNA

1958 Meselson and Stahl demonstrate the nature of DNA replication

1961 Crick and Brenner show how base pairs define amino acids

1968 First synthesis of a virus by Arthur Kornberg

1973 Har Khorama makes the first synthetic gene

1977 Itateva synthesizes the human growth hormone

1981 Professor Illmansee clones baby mice

1985 Alec Jefferie develops a method of 'fingerprinting' with DNA

1987 Genetically engineered plants first developed

1989 Seven cloned calves born from same embryo

1991 Sex of a mouse changed at the embryo stage

GENETICS

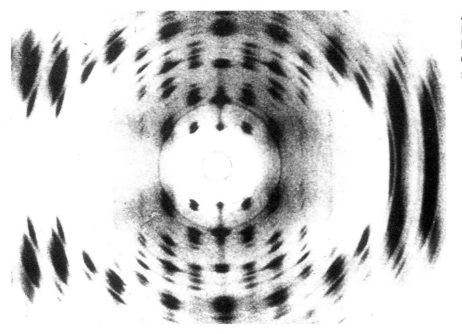

An X-ray diffraction picture of the DNA molecule. An image like this helped James Watson and Francis Crick to unravel the double helix structure of DNA.

THE SHAPE

In 1953 at King's College in London, Maurice Wilkins and Rosalind Franklin were working on passing X-rays through DNA. When X-rays are passed through DNA the rays are scattered. These resulting X-ray diffraction patterns give clues about the physical arrangement of the particles making up DNA. Wilkins and Franklin's results were recorded on film and the photograph showed that DNA was a long, thin molecule coiled in a spiral, or **helix**.

THE DOUBLE HELIX

James Watson and Francis Crick of the Cavendish Laboratory in Cambridge, England used all of these pieces of information to solve the puzzle in 1953. Watson and Crick thought that Chargaff's Rules probably meant that base A was always paired with base T and that base G was always paired with base C. This could only happen if DNA was made up from two strands twisted together to form a 'double helix'.

They built a model which showed that the DNA molecule could be thought of as being a ladder where the bases form the rungs and the sugar and phosphoric acid make up the two sides. The sides are then twisted to make the double-helix.

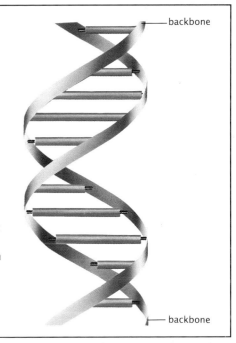

backbone

backbone

SOLVING THE PUZZLE

A COMPLEX MOLECULE

The DNA double-helix is *extremely* small, but if extended, the length of DNA from just one cell is close to one metre! If all the DNA strands from one human being were laid end to end, they would reach from the Earth to the sun and back 50 times!

The DNA molecule

Key
P phosphate
S sugar
G guanine
A adenine
T thymine
C cytosine

sugar-phosphate backbone   inter-linking bases   sugar-phosphate backbone

ONE THOUSAND PAIRS

The length of genes varies, but on average a gene will consist of about 1000 pairs of bases. The 46 chromosomes each consist of tightly coiled, double-helix DNA which holds all of the genetic information needed to define new cells in all their many types and functions.

Unzipping a double helix

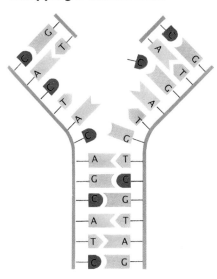

PAIRING UP

James Watson and Francis Crick also decided that the order in which the bases occurred in DNA might be important in making up the code of the genetic information. Also, because the bases could only pair up in a specific manner (G–C, A–T) they knew that the two strands must be **complementary**.

This means that the sequence of bases on one strand makes a pair with, or is the complement of, the sequence of bases in the other strand. As base A is always paired with base T, if A occurs on one strand the complementary base must be T. Once you know the sequence of one strand you can accurately tell the sequence of the other.

HOW DNA COPIES ITSELF

Watson and Crick suggested that the DNA was capable of unwinding itself and 'unzipping' itself into two separate strands. Each strand could then act as a pattern to grow another complementary strand. When the unwinding and the new growth was complete the result would be two DNA molecules. The strands of the new DNA would be built up from a new strand plus one of the old, parental strands.

WORKING IN GROUPS

In 1961, basing their ideas on the gene being a series of base pairs along the DNA molecule, Francis Crick working with Sydney Brenner showed that the pairs of genes worked in groups of three. These groups make up the code for substances known as **amino acids**. The order in which these groups occur decides what information is in the **genetic code**.

THE GENETIC CODE

Between 1961 and 1964 further experiments were carried out which resulted in the genetic code being completely worked out.

The results suggested that as there were four bases which combined in groups of three, it was possible to have 64 groups. These groups were named **codons**. Sixty-one of these groups represent one of the 20 amino acids found in cells. These 20 amino acids are common to *all* living organisms. The other three codons are the equivalent of full-stops at the end of a genetic 'sentence'.

HOW THE GENETIC INFORMATION IS USED

The way DNA was used had still to be explained. The DNA is found in in a cell's nucleus, but a new cell is made outside the nucleus in the cytoplasm. So information about the new cell has to be transferred from the nucleus, where it is stored, to where a new cell can be manufactured. This work is done by another type of nucleic acid (like DNA), called **ribonucleic acid** or

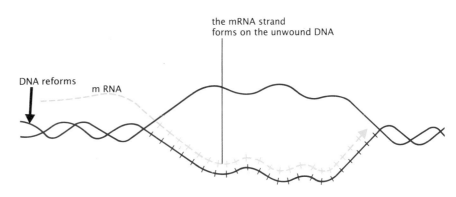

the mRNA strand forms on the unwound DNA

DNA reforms

m RNA

Messenger RNA (mRNA) carries information about the DNA structure to the factories in the cytoplasm. The mRNA is formed when the DNA spiral partially unwinds. After the mRNA strand had been formed the DNA strand reforms.

RNA. RNA molecules are present in all cells where proteins are being made.

A type of RNA known as messenger RNA (mRNA) carries genetic information from the DNA out of the nucleus to the cell 'factory' in the cytoplasm. Part of the DNA double-helix unwinds and one strand acts as a pattern to copy a complementary strand of mRNA which then unzips itself from the DNA. The DNA double-helix returns to its normal state and the mRNA moves out of the nucleus to the cytoplasm. Once in the cytoplasm a second RNA, called transfer RNA, carries it to the 'factory' to be assembled into new proteins.

DNA AND THE GENE

This 'simple' molecule has turned out to be very complex. The earlier problem of how it could carry all of the information needed to code such complicated structures as humans, is no longer a problem. Rather, we seem to have too much DNA coding! As our understanding of the functions of genes and our ability to put them in order, or **sequence** them, improves all the time, we have found that most genes have far more DNA in them than is needed to code the amino acids used in protein production. These lengths of **non-coding DNA** have no known function at present. Similarly, long stretches of the chromosomes seem to be free of any genetic information at all.

A COMPLEX MOLECULE

SELECTION

Species can be defined as groups, called **races**, which are able to cross breed, or interbreed. Slightly different forms are produced but they are still members of the same species. These races are thought to occur when something happens to restrict the exchange of genes in a breeding group. This change can be geographical, climatic or reproductive. It would mean that separated groups of the same species would gradually drift apart, or diverge, genetically. This genetic drift would be due to mutation and the demands of their different environments. Eventually, races can diverge to such an extent that interbreeding is no longer possible. A different species will have been created.

This cow is being fertilized artificially. The sperm has been taken from a prize bull so the calves will have the desired characteristics of either high milk yield or heavy carcasses.

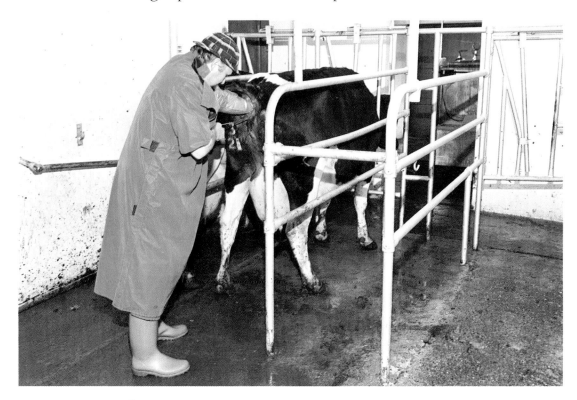

SELECTED CHANGE

People have, sometimes deliberately and other times accidentally, forced unnatural selection on other species. For example our domestic animals, such as cats and dogs and our sheep and cattle, have been bred from wild animals. The animals which showed the characteristics most suitable for tame animals were selected to breed from. Nearly all of our cereals, fruits and vegetables were also developed by a more or less unconscious selection process which began more than 2000 years ago.

GENETICS

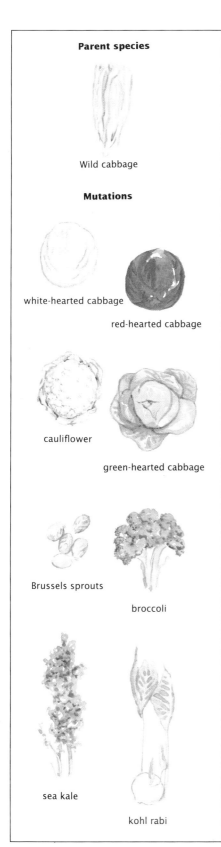

Parent species

Wild cabbage

Mutations

white-hearted cabbage

red-hearted cabbage

cauliflower

green-hearted cabbage

Brussels sprouts

broccoli

sea kale

kohl rabi

Rats have become immune to certain rat poisons. Controlling their numbers is a serious problem because rats are very intelligent and difficult to trap. They are also very destructive and can carry diseases that are fatal to humans.

All these varieties of vegetables have been developed by selective breeding from the original wild cabbage. This is a very long process which can be speeded up by genetic engineering.

RESISTANT STRAINS

In humans there is increasing concern that the frequent use of antibiotics, like penicillin, has created resistant strains of diseases such as tuberculosis, typhoid and cholera. Although new antibiotics have been introduced, they too may cause the same problems.

ACCIDENTAL CHANGE

Selection can also be accidental. It arises from environmental changes that allow a 'stronger' group to breed successfully and dominate a 'weaker' group which may even die out. This strength lies in the genes' reaction to change.

In recent years, chemicals such as **antibiotics**, used to control diseases, and **pesticides**, used mainly to control insects, have been very widely used. Their use has led to changes in some species.

Using the pesticide DDT on insect populations has resulted in a strain of insects which are increasingly immune to DDT. This is because those insects who were more resistant to DDT had a greater chance of living and being able to breed another genetically resistant generation. The pesticide itself did not directly cause the mutation. Similarly, the widespread use of rat poisons like Warfarin have also helped to breed a race of rats which is unaffected by Warfarin.

37

SELECTION

A NEW BRANCH OF GENETICS

The artificial improvement of animals and plants is still going on but in an increasingly scientific and deliberate manner. With our knowledge of how genetics works new methods can be developed. The early 1970s began an exciting time in genetics when methods of selection and hybridization allowed the combinations of genes to be altered. This was the start of the new science of **genetic engineering.**

Combining DNA

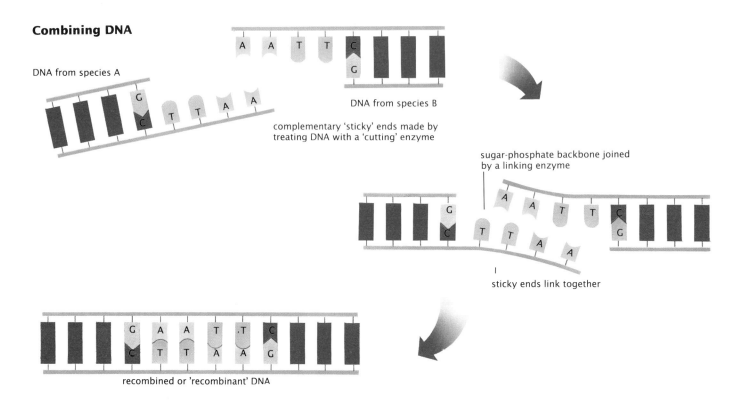

DNA from species A

DNA from species B

complementary 'sticky' ends made by treating DNA with a 'cutting' enzyme

sugar-phosphate backbone joined by a linking enzyme

sticky ends link together

recombined or 'recombinant' DNA

These diagrams show how strands of DNA can be cut and recombined to form new DNA strands which have a desired characteristic like disease resistance.

GENETIC ENGINEERING

An exciting breakthrough was the discovery of enzymes which could cut or break DNA at a particular point. These enzymes made it possible to combine pieces of DNA from different species. Many hundreds of these enzymes have been isolated from cultures of bacteria. They all cut DNA at different places to make either a sticky or a blunt end. The sticky ends of one type of DNA will join with another type of DNA which has a complementary base pairing at its own sticky end. This forms a new, recombined DNA molecule. These recombined DNA molecules can be used to engineer plants with new characteristics such as disease resistance.

COPYING PLANTS

For many years, gardeners have made exact copies of some plants by cutting a stem from the plant, planting the stem in a suitable soil and growing a whole new plant from the cut piece. This **cloning** is such an ordinary process that we think nothing of it, but in a human it would be like growing a new person from a severed finger!

These rows of oil palm plants were cloned in Britain using advanced plant-cell techniques to replicate the best oil palms. When the seedlings were three months old, they were shipped to Malaysia to grow in their warm, native climate.

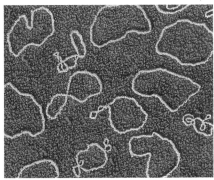

Plasmids like these are circular molecules of DNA that can replicate on their own in a bacterium. The plasmids can be cut to introduce new DNA as required.

CLONING

New techniques developed by **biotechnologists** have taken cloning a stage further. Now whole plants can be regrown from single cells which have been taken from a tiny piece of the original plant. These cells are then put on a growing medium until they form minute plant embryos with buds, leaves or roots. The embryos can be coated with a medium that makes a protective outer case and can then be sown in the ground. With this method large numbers of a plant can be prepared for a farmer in a very short time.

Plants carrying genes for particular features can be cloned by transferring recombined DNA. This can be carried from one species to another by circular molecules, known as DNA **plasmids**, which are found in many types of bacteria. By transferring recombined DNA, biotechnologists can quickly grow new strains of plants which are tolerant to drought, immune to disease or insects, or resistant to chemical **herbicides**, which are used to attack plant diseases.

A NEW BRANCH OF GENETICS

USES OF GENETIC ENGINEERING

Crops are frequently sprayed with pesticides and herbicides to kill insects and weeds that will affect their growth. Sometimes the chemicals in the herbicides are absorbed by the crop. This can be a problem when people or animals become ill if they eat the crop.

Genetic engineering means that whole crops can be grown that are resistant to the effects of a herbicide. Spraying the whole crop will only kill non-resistant weeds and leave the crop unaffected. However, many people are worried that this will lead to the introduction of even more dangerous chemicals into the environment. The manufacturers of pesticides and herbicides disagree, saying that these new developments mean that farmers can now choose herbicides which will not harm people or the environment.

This mouse foetus is being injected with genetic material before it is put back inside its mother to grow normally.

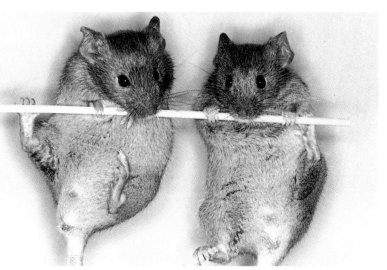

These male mice started their existence as females.

SELF-DEFENCE

Genetic engineering may be able to produce plants that can look after themselves and do not need insecticides. In 1987 scientists in Belgium and the USA added a gene into a tobacco plant. This gene made the plant produce a substance that was poisonous to a type of caterpillar which normally ate tobacco plants.

IMPROVING SPECIES

Genetic engineers can take the fertilized zygote of an animal when it is a single cell and inject new DNA sequences into the zygote. Not many zygotes survive this treatment, but those that do are put back into the animal. The embryo then grows normally as a genetically altered version of the animal. This can result in, say for cattle, increased milk yields or better meat when genes are added which are coded in these areas. In 1991 a similar technique was used to change the sex of a fertilized mouse embryo.

GENETICS

PREVENTING DISEASES

Genetic engineering is also used to prevent diseases. It is used to make **vaccines**, which are dead or weakened forms of germs that cause diseases. The body responds to a vaccine by making antibodies in the blood. These are cells which fight against intruders. So when the actual disease is encountered, the body is ready to fight it.

However, making a vaccine usually means that cells of the disease must be grown. Unfortunately germs causing some diseases, such as hepatitis B, are dangerous to grow artifically. Genetic engineering can sometimes help. Biologists can take the gene with the code that makes the outer, surface protein of the disease and place it in a growing medium. The newly-grown surface protein appears to be like the disease itself but is harmless. After it is taken out of the medium it can be easily and safely purified for use as a vaccine.

MAKING MEDICINES

These genetic techniques have also made it possible to produce important medicines such as insulin for diabetes, or somatostatin for height problems.

Somatostatin, the human growth hormone, was first made in a laboratory in 1977. It is used to help people who are abnormally small grow taller.

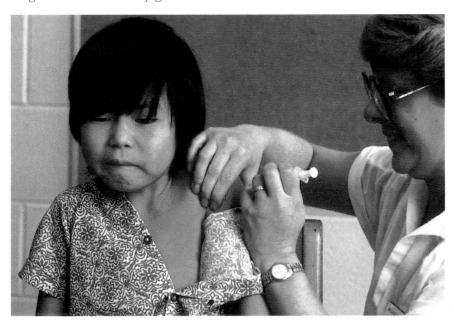

This young Vietnamese child is receiving a pre-school cocktail of vaccinations for diseases like measles, smallpox and diptheria.

GENETIC DISEASES

DNA techniques are particularly useful in diagnosing and perhaps treating genetic diseases. There are more than 3000 of these diseases known to be caused by defects in single genes.

Tests to detect a disease can be made on the embryo in a pregnant woman. Doctors do not touch the embryo but take a small piece of tissue around it for their tests. These pieces of tissue can be used to detect such diseases as muscular dystrophy, cystic fibrosis and sickle-cell anaemia, all of which are inherited.

USES OF GENETIC ENGINEERING

Moral Issues in Genetics

When the results of early genetic engineering were made public in the 1970s, many people became worried about whether engineering could cause different strains of a disease to occur. These might prove to be more dangerous than the original!

Geneticists used to believe that cross-species animals like this 'ligon' female (which was the result of artificially crossing a tiger and a lion) were infertile and couldn't have children. This female proved them wrong and had a baby on April 17 1984 in Thoiry zoo in France.

Setting up Guidelines

In the USA, public concern was so great that all research in genetic engineering was halted between 1974 and 1976. Then a set of guidelines were published which set out to control the possible dangers. Most countries now have similar guidelines. It was not until 1985 that genetically engineered organisms, in the form of pesticides, were first legally released into the environment.

FUTURE BENEFITS

There is still a lot of public concern about such issues as human **gene therapy**. In this technique, which is still very experimental, diseased cells are taken from a patient, the DNA is altered, and the cells replaced in the patient. Such methods have had limited success in animals, but the most exciting prospect is that of actually curing a genetic disease at the embryo stage.

These calves were all grown from one egg from a prize cow which had been fertilized by sperm from a prize bull. The calves are all genetically identical and their embryos will be used to breed more identical and perfect offspring.

A LONG TERM PROJECT

Much is now understood about DNA and the gene but much more remains to be discovered. In 1991 a meeting in London of geneticists from all over the world started a 15-year project to isolate all the genes in the human being and define how they work.

FUTURE DANGERS

When altering DNA scientists are concerned to check that there is no danger that other genes may be accidentally altered or damaged.

There is, however, a danger that once the human gene sequence is finally understood, the knowledge could be used to create genetically designed people – to breed people selectively. It is possible that genetic engineering could change human beings mentally or physically and so change our world. In the future, genetics will only be of benefit to us if the science is used intelligently in a mature, sensible society.

MORAL ISSUES IN GENETICS

KEY DATES

1665 Robert Hooke discovers the cell

1754 Pierre Maupertuis suggests species transform over time

1802 Jean-Baptiste Lamarck gives biology its name

1809 Lamarck's book *Philosophie zoologique* published

1824 René Dutrochet discovers that tissue is made from living cells

1831 Charles Darwin sets out on his voyage on the *Beagle*

1833 Robert Brown discovers the cell nucleus

1858 Charles Darwin publishes his results

1859 Darwin publishes *On the Origin of Species by Natural Selection*

1865 Gregor Mendel discovers the laws of segregation

1868 Freidrich Miescher discovers nuclein, later renamed DNA

1888 G Waldyer names the 'chromosome'

1891 Henking describes sex chromosomes and autosomes

1901 Hugo de Vries first describes mutations

1902 Walter Sutton publishes the *Chromosome Theory of Inheritance*

1907 First culture 'in vitro' of animal cells by R Harrison

1909 Wilhelm Johannsen first uses the name 'gene' and Garrod suggests that errors in genes lead to hereditary disorders

1910 Thomas Hunt Morgan discovers the sex-linked gene

1926 Morgan's book, *The Theory of the Gene,* published

1927 Hermann Muller shows that X-rays cause mutation

1937 Richard Goldschmidt discovers genes exist as points along the chromosome

1944 Avery, MacCarty, and Macleod suggest that DNA is involved in the hereditary material

1950 Chargaff's Rules established about the basic chemistry of DNA

1952 Hershey and Chase prove that DNA is the hereditary material, and Wilkins and Franklin take X-ray diffraction pictures of DNA

1953 Crick and Watson discover the structure of DNA

1957 Arthur Kronberg shows the 'unzipping' of DNA

1958 Meselson and Stahl demonstrate the nature of DNA replication

1961 Crick and Brenner show how base pairs define amino acids

1968 First synthesis of a virus by Arthur Kornberg

1973 Har Khorama makes the first synthetic gene

1977 Itateva synthesizes the human growth hormone

1981 Professor Illmansee clones baby mice

1985 Alec Jefferie develops a method of 'fingerprinting' with DNA

1987 Genetically engineered plants first developed

1989 Seven cloned calves born from same embryo

1991 Sex of a mouse changed at the embryo stage

GENETICS

GLOSSARY

acid: one of the three fundamental chemical substances that form all chemicals. Acids contain hydrogen gas which they give off in water to create a reaction. Acids have a sour taste

amino acids: simple units found in living things. They combine together to make up enzymes and proteins

antibiotics: chemical substances which destroy bacteria. They are used as medicine

antibodies: proteins in the body fluid which defend the body against disease. Antibodies are made by white blood cells

autosomes: all chromosomes which do not determine the sex of a plant or animal

backcrossed: a plant fertilized using the pollen from a parent plant not displaying its own characteristic ie tall backcrossed with a short

bacteria: the single-celled organisms found everywhere. Some cause disease but others break down waste matter

base: one of three fundamental chemical substances. Bases are the chemical opposite of an acid as they accept particles of hydrogen gas

biotechnologists: scientists who specialize in the field of advanced studies into living organisms

carrier: an organism with a gene that causes a variation in some of its young. The gene is recessive and can only dominate in certain conditions. The carrier is unaffected by the gene

cells: the basic units that make up living things and carry out all its functions

centromere: the small pinched in area at the centre of a chromosome. Chromosomes divide at the centromere

characteristic: a distinguishing feature or quality

chemical analysis: the study of the substances that make up an organism and the observation of their reactions together

chromosomes: the thread-like structures in the nucleus of all cells. They carry information about the nature and function of the cell

classification: a way of grouping similar types of animals or plants

cloning: a way of producing new organisms without sexual reproduction

codon: a combination of any three of the four bases which make up DNA

complementary: used to describe something which makes something else complete. The two strands of DNA are complementary

cosmic rays: radiation from space. It is absorbed by all living things on Earth

cytoplasm: the jelly-like material surrounding the nucleus of a cell. It contains the factories that make the chemicals needed by the cell

deoxyribonucleic acid (DNA): one of two acids found in the nuclei of cells. DNA is made up of many individual units laid out like two chains attached by rungs. The chains are twisted around each other

dominant: used to describe something that controls or is stronger than something else

epigenesis: the theory, which most people believe, that an embryo gradually develops its specialised parts (eg arms and fingers) as it grows, unlike the preformation theory which thought that all the parts were there in miniature from the beginning (ie pre-formed)

embryo: an undeveloped creature or plant such as the young of an animal before being born or hatched

evolution: the process of gradually developing or changing

experiment: a controlled test to find out what happens, especially in science

F1 hybrid: the first generation of young made from parents of different types or varieties

fertilize: to enable a living thing to produce young

fixed ratio: a fixed number of times that one thing occurs in relation to another

gametes: the units in living things that join together to form young. In humans the gametes are the sperm and the egg

genera (*sing.* **genus**): a group of similiar animals or plants

generation: a) a group of people who are of roughly the same age, such as children, parents, grandparents; b) the child or children of each age group as in children, parents, grandparents, etc

genes: the coded instructions for the appearance and make-up of a living thing

gene therapy: altering the genetic code in diseased cells to repair genetic defects

genetic code: the pattern of genes which carries the instructions for each cell's function

GLOSSARY

genetic engineering: the science of altering genetic codes in the cells of living things to produce a change

helix: a spiral shape

herbicides: a chemical substance that is used to destroy weeds and other unwanted plants

heredity: the passing of similarities of appearance or physical habit from parent to child

homologue: something that has the same structure as its partner

hybrid: made from parents of two different types or varieties

inherit: to receive qualities from a parent or grandparent

insight: a sudden understanding or idea

medium: a substance containing a suitable food source for the growth of a plant or other organism

meiosis: when the nucleus of a cell divides to produce sex cells which have only half the number of chromosomes found in a complete cell

mitosis: when a cell in a plant or animal divides for growth or to repair damage. When the cell divides each cell carries the same amount of information about the cell's function as the original cell

modified: used to describe something that has been changed in some way

molecule: the smallest possible unit of a chemical compound

mutagenic: used to describe something which causes something to mutate

mutation: something that is different from its parents, usually in appearance or behaviour

non-coding: not carrying any genetic messages

nucleus: the control centre of a cell in an animal or plant

offspring: children of humans or animals, and seedlings of plants

organism: anything that is living and can have a separate existence

pesticides: a chemical substance which destroys insects

phage: something which 'eats' or absorbs something else. Phages use bacteria as hosts in which to reproduce

plant-hybridization: breeding plants with parents from different types or varieties

plasmid: a small circular unit found in the area surrounding the nucleus in a bacteria cell. Plasmids can carry genetic information from one species to another

pollen: tiny grains produced by the male parts of flowers which are carried to the female parts by the wind or insects to fertilize the female

proteins: a group of substances which are the basis of every cell. Proteins are very complex and are made up of hundred or thousands of simple units called amino acids

race: a group connected by common distinguishing features

rational: used to describe something that is sensible or thought out

recessive: used to describe something that is pushed back or fades away

replication: to make an exact copy of something

reproduce: to make more of the same, such as children or new plants

ribonucleic acid (RNA): one of two acids found in the cell nuclei of living organisms. RNA is a single spiral with rungs, rather like a ladder cut in half down its length

selfing: used to describe a plant that uses its own pollen to fertilize itself

self-pollination: using a plant's own pollen to fertilize itself

sequence: to put in the correct order, one after another

sex chromosomes: the chromosomes that are contributed by the male and female to their offspring. There are two types: the X and the Y chromosomes

sex-linked genes: genes on an X chromosome which do not have a matching partner on the paired Y chromosome in a male cell.

species: a similar type of animal or plant

sperm: short form of spermatozoa, tiny organisms in fluid produced by male animals. When a sperm combines with a female egg, the female has children

spontaneous: used to describe something that happens without planning

sterile: a) free from germs; b) unable to produce seeds or young

successive: used to describe things that come one after another

systematic: used to describe something that is well planned or organized

theory: an idea based on reasoned thinking to explain certain facts

tissue: the material which plants and animals are made of

vaccine: a weakened version of a disease-causing virus that is given to enable a human or animal resist the full strength disease

variability: being able to change

X chromosome: one of the two sex chromosomes. Females have two X chromosomes, males only have one

Y chromosome: one of the two sex chromosomes. Y chromosomes are only found in males, paired with, but smaller than, an X chromosome

zygote: the first cell of a new animal made from a male and a female sex cell joining together

BIBLIOGRAPHY

Introducing Genetics, R N Jones and A Karp (John Murray 1986)
The Book of Inventions and Discoveries, V-A Giscard d'Estaing (ed) (Macdonald Queen Anne Press 1990)

FURTHER READING

The Science of Genetics, George W Burns & Paul J Bottino (Collier Macmillan 1989)
Genetics, Monroe W Stickberger (Collier Macmillan 1985)
The Cell Concept, L M J Kramer & J K Scott (Macmillan 1989)
Heredity, Development & Evolution, Christine Birkett (Macmillan 1987)

GLOSSARY

INDEX

GENETICS